To the Arlington's,

May the grace and peace of Christ be with you as you enter the next chapter in your life.

Aloha!

The Yamashiros

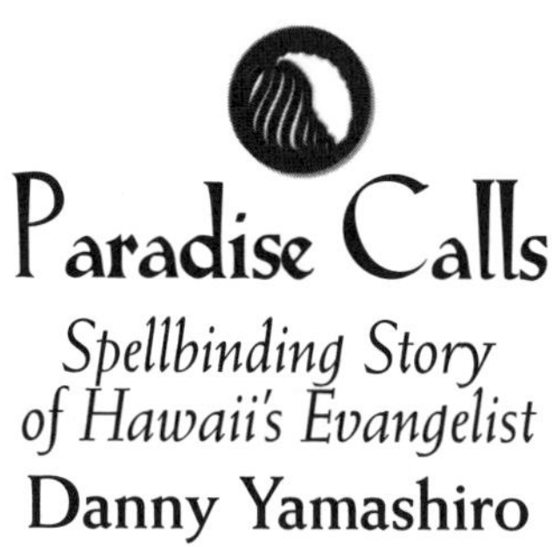

Paradise Calls

Spellbinding Story of Hawaii's Evangelist

Danny Yamashiro

Honolulu, Hawaii

Paradise Calls
Spellbinding Story of Hawaii's Evangelist
Danny Yamashiro

Edited by Jean Tatami
Photography, Cover and Book Design by Joel Dasalla
Japanese Translation by Kazuyo Kitaguchi

Photos courtesy of:
Joel Dasalla
Phil Spalding
Gabriel Wong
Millie Yoshimoto

Dedication

To

Jesus Christ
my
Savior and Lord.

To **Evangeline L.K. Yamashiro,**
who stood by me during the painful isolated years
of my life while Jesus taught me to
find Him in the Scriptures.

To **David T. Yamashiro, Sr.,**
who disciplined me from my childhood with a
God-given awareness that I was created
to serve the Lord.

To **Jamie M.T. Yamashiro,**
who is my faithful, lifelong companion,
understanding so patiently the burden
and call of an evangelist.

Contents

Foreword

by
Daniel I. Kikawa

Within a few minutes of meeting Danny Yamashiro, you know that you are in the presence of an extraordinary individual. His desire for the lost is so tangible that its force seems to knock you backwards. I remember thinking, "How can this man survive without blowing up?" I have met many men and women of God and all have a desire for the lost but I had never met anyone whose desire for the lost overwhelmed me. The energy exploding forth from the man, the burning desire and barely controlled passion to see the lost saved made me ask him, "What made you this way?"

When Danny told me the story of his life, I told him, like many others before me, *"You've got to write a book!"* Well, you are very blessed to have this book in your hands. I also know that you are one of two kinds of people: those who have met Danny and had to read this book or those who are reading the book and will have to meet Danny.

Daniel I. Kikawa
Author
Perpetuated in Righteousness

Preface

Before I formed you in the womb I knew you; before you
were born I sanctified you; and I ordained you a
prophet to the nations
JEREMIAH 1:5

Mamua aku o ka'u hana ana ia oe iloko o ka opu, ike aku no au
ia oe; a mamua aku o kou puk ana mawaho mai o ka opu, hoolaa
aku au ia oe, a hoolilo no au ia oe i kaula no na lahuikanaka.
IEREMIA I:5

This story is to present Christ. It is also a program of the Holy Spirit as effected through me. I believe God has opened a door. He has directed me to describe how I came to know Jesus Christ, and how through a dramatic, nearly tragic mountain climbing accident, I was called into the ministry of evangelistic preaching.

He has inspired, protected, reproved, disciplined and guided me. I am convinced that apart from Christ my life would have little meaning and purpose. It has always been a delight to share about God's grace and miraculous work in my life.

The fact that my sins have been forgiven through His sacrifice on the cross and the fact that He was raised from

the dead and lives today have radically influenced my life,
changing my perspective on my reason for existence.
I write as a man burdened for people to know Jesus as
Savior and Lord. My heart's yearning is to share with
Hawaii and the world, the loving and saving message of
Christ crucified, risen, and soon coming King.

My prayer is that you will be blessed by how the Lord
has mercifully and gently dealt with me, a sinner needing
His forgiveness; a desperate man longing for God's touch
on my life so that I may be useful for His service. May He
reveal Himself to you in transforming ways you did not
know before, and to that end may His grace and love
be poured into your heart.

Danny Yamashiro
Honolulu, Hawaii
1997

I

Called from Childhood

子 供 時 代

But they that wait upon the Lord shall renew their strength; they shall mount up with wings as eagles, they shall run and not be weary, they shall walk and not faint.
ISAIAH 40:31

Aka, o ka poe hilinai aku ia Iehova, e ulu hou no ko lakou ikaika; Epii eheu aku no lakou iluna, e like me na aito; E holo no lakou, aole hoi e maloeloe, E hele mua no lakou, aole hoi e maule.
ISAIA XL:31

Paradise Calls

My parents gave me the name Daniel Keauhou Matsu Yamashiro when I was born on December 5, 1967. Daniel came from the Hebrew name meaning "God is my judge," Keauhou is a Hawaiian name meaning, "A new beginning, a new era," Matsu was my grandfather's name and is the Japanese word for "Pine or pine tree" symbolizing strength and Yamashiro means "Castle on the mountain." Those names all hold special meaning to me as I have seen parts of each throughout my life.

When I was eight, I sat beside my father, David T. Yamashiro, Sr. in our big blue Buick Le Sabre. It was 1975 and we lived in quiet Moanalua Gardens of Honolulu. Dad had been telling me Bible stories about Jesus as early as I could remember. Often, I would eagerly ask him, "Daddy, tell me a Jesus story!" There was a desire in me to know Jesus.

The crucifixion of Jesus was before me as my father had bought a picture of Christ on the cross during one of his business trips to Guam. Another picture I remember was one of a shepherd reaching over a treacherous cliff, risking his life to rescue a sheep that was lost and entangled by the bush. Those pictures became increasingly significant as the years passed. I understood that Jesus loved me and that He died on the cross for my sins. I was made conscious of Christ's shed blood as my mother, Evangeline L.K. Yamashiro, whose ancestry was Hawaiian and Chinese, knelt beside my bed thanking Him in her nightly prayers for "covering me with His precious blood." I knew He was raised from the dead. I believed He would come again. It was simple. I wanted to be close to Him. I wanted to know Him.

In the garage that afternoon in 1975, my father simply asked me if I wanted to receive Jesus Christ as my Lord and Savior. I said yes. He led me in prayer. I repeated the words, "Jesus, thank you for dying for my sins. Please forgive me of my sins. I receive You into my heart as my Savior and Lord." It was the beginning of my personal relationship with Jesus Christ.

This was a sign to me of Christ's call on my life. In

those early years, the senior minister at Kalihi Union
Church was a gentle, loving pastor named Dr. Stanley
Johnson. I was strangely intrigued by the presence of
such godly men like him. Their tenderness exemplified
Christ, it was not weak but strong. I wanted to be like
Christ and I wanted to be a minister.

I had a quiet, lonely childhood. I was the youngest.
Deva was the oldest, then David, Jr., and my second
sister Iolani. Iolani and I were eight years apart. I had
much time to myself, and became a dreamer. At
Moanalua Elementary and Iolani School, my parents
received reports from teachers that I was a day-dreamer.
Staring out the window was a joy to me. I felt like I
could travel the world and meet people in my dreams.
I also found that my thoughts were not always
good thoughts.

I began to learn that I had a difficult time consis-
tently doing what I knew God wanted me to do. My
behavior at the elementary school was not consistent
with my behavior at home. I had learned to curse and

conduct myself in unacceptable ways. I lived a dual life, learning to hide what was really happening from my parents, and that showed me the capacity I had to be deceitful.

I knew that the Lord would forgive me if I confessed. Before I reached the age of nine, I had learned to close my door, kneel beside my bed and ask for forgiveness. There were even moments when I would plead with God as I knelt, begging Him to help me overcome my sins.

The more I learned to read, the more I sought to read my Bible. My favorite color was white, because it was the color of purity. My father had given me a white King James Bible as a gift and I tried reading it everyday. There was something very special about it. I knew I was reading a supernatural book that had the power to change me.

When I have looked back at baby pictures, I have noticed that my father had put a Bible beside my head when I slept. The Bible has never been an ordinary book to me and I have grown to love it more each day. In it, God speaks to me and the Holy Spirit draws me closer to Jesus.

Nobody knew that I was learning to walk with the Lord because I wanted to keep it a secret. I did not want anyone to know that I desired to be like Jesus. Somehow, it did not seem "cool."

I was aware that the Lord knew me and I knew Him. I understood that there was more to my relationship with Him than just going to church. Although I could not say it in words, I had an awareness that He had called me to serve Him. As I reflect on significant moments in the earlier years, I recall a special love for the words in Isaiah 40:31.

It became my life verse. There was a certain security in the Lord I found in that Scripture. It was both majestic and affirming. It was hopeful and strengthening. There was a promise from the Lord in that passage. If I waited upon Him, my strength would be renewed. That is, my strength would come from him. He would enable me to run and not be weary, to walk and not faint, to live for him as I so wanted to, deep in my heart.

I had a love for the song that put those words to music, which ended, "Teach me Lord, teach me Lord to wait." The Lord answered my prayer and continued to teach me to wait upon Him. There would be moments in the years to follow, when I was reminded by God's Spirit about His promise for me if I waited upon Him.

II

Called through Shattered Dreams

打ち砕かれた夢の中

*And Elijah came to all the people, and said,
"How long will you falter between two opinions? If
the Lord is God, follow Him; but if Baal,
then follow him."*
I KINGS 18:21

*Hele mai la hoi o Elia i ka poe kanaka a pau, i mai
la hoi, Pehea la ka loihi o ko oukou kapekepeke ana
iwaena o na manao elua? Ina o Iehova ke Akua, e
hahai oukou mamuli ona; aka, ina o Baala, e hahai
mamuli ona. Aile olelo aku na kanaka i kekahi
olelo ia ia.*
NA LII I XVIII:21

I had a dream. It was to become a great football player. My father had been a spectacular half-back player making the All-Star team in 1950 at Iolani School
under the legendary Father Kenneth A. Bray. My older
brother received All-State honors in 1975 as a defensive
back at Radford High School and later received a full
scholarship to the University of Hawaii. My dream was
not only to be like them, but to supersede them.

I had an early start. My playing for the Kalakaua
Monarchs in Kalihi enabled me to develop basic skills
as a hopeful player. Every day, my coach Glen Johansen
would pick me up and take me to practice. Coach Glen
and coach Reuben Ka'ahanui treated the team as their
own sons, teaching us discipline and respect. I was both
a quarterback and a defensive back. My performance
was promising.

After four years with Kalakaua, I decided to play for
Iolani's intermediate team. I had a very discouraging
season in my attempt at adjusting to the Interscholastic
League of Honolulu (ILH). The boys were bigger and I

was slow in growing. I did not perform well, lost my starting position and wanted to quit playing football. The Junior Varsity football coach, Chucky Nakoa encouraged me to play for him and be "his quarterback." I decided to give it another try. I was privileged to train with Hawaii's best football players. My best friend, Hugh Dunn and I ran to the University of Hawaii to workout with Blane Gaison, a former Hula Bowl MVP and a cornerback for the Atlanta Falcons, Tim Lyons who was UH's starting quarterback, and others who would dedicate themselves to running up the awesome Wilhemina Rise in Kaimuki every single day. We later learned more techniques from the defensive back Richard Miano, another UH great who played for the New York Jets.

My JV season, as a freshman, was a losing one although I learned valuable leadership skills. As a tenth grader, I was one of three sophomores to make the varsity squad under Head Coach Eddie Hamada. I discovered two things. First, my relationship with Christ

became distant as I chased my dream that brought
attention, popularity, and hope for self-glory in the
future. Second, my performance was not as impressive
as I had expected.

But, there was hope. My junior year was a high.
Several interceptions and a few touchdowns, along with
refining my techniques in hitting and tackling, quickly
built my confidence. Then, at the Aloha Stadium,
returning a kickoff against Damien High School my left
foot got stuck in the astroturf when I tried to "cut
back." My body turned as my foot remained planted in
the turf and my cartilage and ligament tore. I was out
for the season. Knee surgery was required under
the skillful hands of orthopedic surgeon Dr. Allen
Richardson.

During my senior year I disappointingly became the
only one of three captains who did not finish the season. On a punt return against Kamehameha Schools,
the same thing happened, and my left knee buckled.

Anger, hurt, bitterness, and fear piled on me. My

grades in school were unsatisfactory and my career as an athlete was jeopardized. At the age of seventeen, I began to retreat to some reclusive tendencies I had developed as a child. The relationship with my parents began to sour as I outwardly rebelled. I felt comfortable being alone, safe. Searching for a way to fill the emptiness I had thoughts of running away from home. My grades were poor and I feared the shame of flunking from such a prestigious institution as Iolani School.

At a math exam in which I went unprepared, I spent the time writing a goodbye note to my parents. I felt trapped and thought that the only way for me was to run. I wanted independence. Hiking became a way of escape for me. I often took long walks into the early hours of the morning as well as during the day.

In all this, the Lord was taking away something I deemed precious in order to give me that which was eternally invaluable—a close relationship with Him that required total devotion. Missionary martyr Jim Elliot said, "He is no fool who gives up what he cannot keep to gain what he cannot lose." Christ loved me so much that He would not allow me to continue compromising devotion to Him and devotion to a sport. I was being called from football to another specific area of work which would require as much and more commitment. This shift is not to state that no person can truly love and serve God while excelling in athletics. Many have done so exceedingly well. In this instance, however, it has become a conviction that applies to me, personally.

III

Called from a 400 Foot Fall

４００フィートの転落

And when I passed by you and saw you struggling in your own blood, I said to you in your blood, "Live!" Yes, I said to you in your blood, "Live!" . . . "Yes, I swore an oath to you and entered into a covenant with you and you became Mine," says the Lord God. Then I washed you in water; yes, I thoroughly washed off your blood, and I anointed you with oil.
EZEKIEL 16:6,8-9

A maalo ae la au ma ou la, a ike ia oe e paumaele ana i kou koko iho, i aku la au ia oe iloko o kou koko, E ola; oiaio, ua olelo aku au ia oe iloko o kou koko, E ola.
EZEKIELA XVI:6

Paradise Calls

I took long hikes alone. One of those was the famed Pali Lookout in Nuuanu. I found a serene haven at the bottom of the Old Pali road. As a senior in high school, I was free to leave campus during my free periods. I would drive to the scenic lookout. I would lie on the deserted pavement praying, thinking, singing. It was a place for me to go and be alone with the Lord. There, I wrestled with unanswered questions and shared my fears with Christ.

I prayed, "Lord, I don't know what's happening to me. I don't know what my life is about. I feel You close to me, but I want to be closer. You're here, but something is blocking. Please bring me close to You. I don't know what it is that will bring me closer. It's near by and I want it."

The next week on Sunday, December 22, 1985, I took my friend Stacy Loui, the girl I was dating, to the same place. Earlier that memorable afternoon, I had prepared the Sunday lunch of "somen" (oriental noodles) for my mother and told her where I was going.

Called from a 400 Foot Fall

She earnestly warned me of the danger, which I had shrugged off.

At the beginning of the hike, we followed a small trail. When the trail ended, we decided to go further by grabbing tree branches, limbs and rocks which came out of the ground. I removed my shirt to "show off" as I scaled a thirty foot rock cliff with no ropes. We hiked deeper and higher up the mountain. After three hours, the sun had set and we attempted to climb over the top of the mountain.

I was climbing directly above Stacy when she apparently grabbed one of the rocks or roots I had loosened. I was about ten feet from the top when she fell 20 feet below me. Miraculously, she landed on a tree stump. She assured me that she was okay, but was stranded with no where to go. She encouraged me to continue climbing to the top which should have led to a trail on the other side. Then, I could call for help.

My refusal to do that was my unwillingness to leave her there alone and the embarrassment of being put on the local television news. I proceeded cautiously to make my way down to rescue her. In my attempt, I slipped and fell 300 feet. She recalls seeing my shadow quietly pass by head first. Not knowing where I had landed, she was incredibly enabled by the Lord to find her way back to the trail and in a little more than an hour's time climb down to the old road where we had started.

Stacy's legs were wet and bleeding. She frantically screamed for help as she ran the four hundred yards uphill to the Lookout. Although the Lookout is typically empty at night, on this particular evening there was an exception. She saw a gathering of people singing as they overlooked the lights and mountains of beautiful Kailua. They were a group from the Youth With A Mission (YWAM) led by the team leader Curtis Van Hulla. The YWAM is a Christian missionary organization based on the Big Island of Hawaii. These young people were on their way to the Philippines for a winter mission. Earlier that day, during a time of worship, the Lord had directed them to "go to the mountain and pray."

When they saw Stacy, they did not panic. They called on the Lord for help and direction. Two of them had visions. One saw a vision of a giant hand catching me. The other saw a giant hand catching me with another hand covering me.

They prayed for the Lord to show them where I had landed. Then they called 911 at the emergency telephone. I heard the story from the perspective of the man who made the call. I asked, "What actually happened, when you called for help?" I learned that during that distressing moment, the Lord was orchestrating His gracious work of salvation.

Curtis Van Hulla, the YWAM team leader explained: "I called for help and the dispatcher told me, 'Nobody could survive a fall that far. Besides it's dark now and since you have no idea where he might be it would be futile to jeopardize the lives of the rescuers. We'll come and pick up his body tomorrow.' But I felt this inspiration and I said to him, 'You must come! I believe he's still alive.'

"Jesus did not come to save the dead, but the living! Just then the dispatcher asked me to hold on. He came back and said, 'Could you tell us even a little about where he was climbing and where he fell?' I gave him as much explanation as possible having gathered details from the girl that was with you. He asked me to hold on once more. He returned to the phone and said, 'We've just completed several days of training in that same part of the mountain. We know the place 'like the back of our hand.' We'll send the team right over."

One officer arrived first. Stacy led the officer to an obscure part of the mountain identified by a patch of ginger plants. She looked up and said, "He's around here somewhere!" Amazingly, I had landed in the dangerously slanted patch which compromised my stability. I lay there unaware that the rescue squad had been summoned and the television news cameras were filming the feared tragic event.

Called from a 400 Foot Fall

It was not possible for the rescuers to reach over the thirty foot cement wall which separated me from them. There was another 100 foot drop. As the men attempted to climb from the sides and grab hold of me, I moved and fell again. This time, the rescue helicopter was called to light the darkened shrubbery, to look for plants which were laid flat, indicating something heavy, such as my body, was there.

The men rappelled to the place where I had landed. Under the light of the helicopter's beam, the men who found me were surprised that I was not lying flat, but was sitting up and moaning. My scalp had ripped off, shredded, hanging off the back of my skull, opened like a peeled banana. My head was cracked, fractured in two places. My body was lacerated in many areas, my left ankle was shattered in three places, and my organs smashed. That body position aided in slowing the flow of blood from my open scalp. In those hours of rescue I had lost too much blood and was in a state of shock. They wrapped my head and tied me into the basket which was carried by the helicopter up to the parking lot of the Lookout.

I was rushed to the St.Francis Hospital's Trauma Room. I spent six hours in emergency surgery. Irma Miller, the head nurse and family friend was called on to do the best she could with my open scalp. She scrubbed the dirt from the inside of my scalp, plucking blades of grass and small pebbles which held the risk of infection.

The doctors and nurses did not expect me to make it through the night. They decided to patch me up as quickly as possible and to let my family see me for the last time. My head was literally the size of a basketball. My eyes were swollen shut. My skin was stretched so tight it glimmered. When family and close friends were given permission to see me, they needed a warning that I would not look the same. I have been told that I was unrecognizable.

I lay in a coma for one week. It was a week of fear and uncertainty for my family. They were forced to watch the respirator make my lungs inhale and exhale as I remained unconscious. The Lord gave them strength through God's promise from Philippians 4:6 which states, *"Be anxious for nothing, but in everything by prayer and supplication, with thanksgiving, let your requests be made known to God; and the peace of God, which surpasses all understanding will guard your hearts and minds through Christ Jesus."*

The next day, the captain of the rescue squad went back to the Lookout to survey the scene of the accident. He told my parents that it was impossible for me to have landed in the ginger patch. My body weight and momentum, the curvature of the mountain, and the fact that there was no wind at the time of the fall made it a miracle for me to have landed in the patch, the only one along the whole road. No other place along the 400 yards would have been able to break my fall. He said, "Mr. and Mrs. Yamashiro, I don't understand it, but it was as if a big hand caught him and placed him there." In Isaiah 41:10, the Lord assured his people,

Paradise Calls

*"So do not fear, for I am with you; do not be dismayed,
for I am your God. I will strengthen you and help you;
I will uphold you with my righteous right hand."*

I remained in the hospital for nearly one month. Dr. Dudley Seto, a high school classmate of my father, oversaw the whole process of medical care. There was concern about my head injury and different therapists came to offer their assistance. My neurosurgeon Dr. Calvin Kam did not require their help. My left ankle was fixed by Dr. Albert Chun Hoon who used two screws to hold the shattered bones together. My forehead and scalp having taken infection required extensive reconstructive surgery. Dr. F. Don Parsa, the plastic surgeon, opened the scalp which was sewn together and successfully attempted to stretch skin to make up for other parts which had been lost.

I left the hospital weighing a meager 120 pounds. It was a big change from my bulky 165 pounds. My hair was shaved off and 70 stitches held my scalp together. My left leg was in a cast up to my knee with over 30 stitches. Additional stitches were on my back, arms and legs. My eyes were swollen and bruised from the surgery. My physical appearance was altered tremendously from the fall.

Never again would I look into the mirror and see the same young man whose body and face were without major scars. My body was forced to age in the process of that traumatic month. The effects of it carried into the years following. And the Lord remembered my prayer. I wanted to be near Him. I wanted to experience a close relationship with my Savior. He allowed me to go through this accident in order to bring me to the place where He wanted me to be - completely broken. It may seem contradictory, but the biblical principle rang true: to truly live, one must die. I could hear Him calling me as the Good Shepherd who came to save me that night at the treacherous Pali Lookout.

It was a "wake up" call. My attitude had been one of hopefulness. I felt that somehow, I would be acceptable to God if I tried my best. At that moment in my life, I realized that without Christ, I was hopeless. My best was not good enough. The deceit, the compromise, the pride, the ambition, the hope in myself revealed my complete sinfulness. Those characteristics were rooted in my inability to please God on my own. I did not have what was needed. I desperately needed someone to help me. That is when the Holy Spirit opened my heart to understand fully the good news of Jesus Christ. There was hope!

I learned that it was not the end for me, but the start of a new beginning. A choice needed to be made. I was at the lowest moment of my young life. Physically, a wreck, emotionally like a child, mentally confused, but spiritually, God was giving me guidance. If I were to continue trying to live for myself, I would be miserable. The Holy Spirit impressed on my heart the need to surrender my life to Christ. The words of Galatians 2:20 applied to me, *"I have been crucified with Christ and I no longer live, but Christ lives in me. The life I live in the body, I live, by faith in the Son of God, who loved me and gave himself for me."* He saved me for a purpose. In order for me to find His purpose , I was required to learn to let Him live through me. To say I receive Jesus as Lord and Savior meant complete submission to Him as Lord and Savior.

On a Sunday in May 1986, I asked my father if he would pray with me. I chose to dedicate my life to Christ in complete surrender. I knelt on the floor of his study and he layed his hands on me. I asked the Lord to take full control of my life. "I'm sorry for my pride and presumption. I choose to repent. Whatever you want me to do, I will do. Wherever you want me to go, I will go. Whatever you want me to say, I will say. I give my life to you. My life is in your hands. Use me to fulfill your dreams, your plans for your honor and glory."

Nearly two months had passed when I drove over the Pali Highway and looked at the mountains that almost engulfed me. It was then that the Spirit of

Paradise Calls

Christ spoke to me. It was not an audible voice, but it was unmistakable. I heard Him in my spirit. He said to me, *"Daniel, I saved you to preach Jesus Christ."* I responded, *"Yes, Lord."* From that moment on, I knew why I was alive. I knew then, as I know now, that I am called to preach Jesus and call people to Him.

IV

Called to New Hopes, New Dreams

新しい希望、新たな夢

Do not remember the former things, nor consider the things of old. Behold I will do a new thing, now it shall spring forth; shall you not know it? I will even make a road in the wilderness and rivers in the desert.
ISAIAH 43:18-19

Mai hoomanao oukou i na mea mamua, Mai manao hoi i na mea kahiko. Aia hoi e hana ana au i mea hou; I keaia manawa no ia e puka mai ai; He oialo no, e hana no wau i alanui ma ka waonahele.
ISAIA XLIII:18-19

Not only were my dreams shattered, my body was torn. Miraculously however, my body healed with amazing rapidness. On the other hand, my emotions were at an upheaval and my spirit was broken. The Lord protected me from brain damage and enabled me to graduate with my class from Iolani School in 1986. Now, I was completely dependent on Him, a crushed young man. This was the time of my spiritual awakening.

I was accepted at Biola University in La Mirada, California to major in Biblical Studies and Theology. As an eighteen year old still recovering from the near fatal accident, my emotions did not enable me to adjust to the separation from my family, my friends, and Hawaii. After one month trying to make it, I had an emotional breakdown. If it were not for my parents who immediately flew to California, I may have committed suicide.

I returned home and was employed by St. Louis Florist, owned by Mr. Ike Akamine, a Spirit-filled man and an elder at our church. The Lord used this time to rebuild me spiritually and emotionally. I gleaned wisdom and insight from godly men such as Mr. Akamine at work, learning from my father at home by watching his example, and listening to Mr. Thomas Masaki, another learned elder, in his expositional studies on the books of John and Revelation. I learned from the consistent and simple faith of Calvin Nakano who discipled Jerry Chang, Joe Inciong, Michael Oshiro, Randall Dunn, Hugh Dunn and me. The Lord enabled me to learn and grow in the wisdom and understanding of Scripture and practical application. I also enjoyed the example of a minister of God's healing in the Reverend Bill Steeper.

In January of 1987, I enrolled at the Chaminade University of Honolulu. It was there that the Lord spoke to me about His anointing for preaching the Gospel. After class one day, I sat in my car reading from the book of Luke chapter 4, verse 18 which said, *"The Spirit of the Lord is upon Me, because He has anointed Me to preach the gospel to the poor. He has sent me to preach deliverance to the captives and recovery of sight to the blind, to set at liberty those who are oppressed, to preach the acceptable year of the Lord."* Jesus was reading a quote from Isaiah 61 and stated that the passage was fulfilled in Him. When I read this, the Holy Spirit impressed on my heart that as a child of God and follower of Jesus, His anointing was on me to preach the Gospel.

The Lord enabled me to achieve excellent grades, showing me a new start in the area of academics. I was surprisingly diligent in my studies. In this time of rebuilding, the Lord put a desire in my heart to give Biola University one more try.

In the fall of 1987, I returned to California to try again where I had failed so miserably the first time. It is common to think that once a person knows what he has been called to do, life becomes easy. But, my first three years away from home were the darkest years of my life. I suffered severe depression and loneliness. There were many nights and days in which I would turn up the volume on my radio, lock my door, and simply wail in my pillow because of the hurt. Nobody but the Lord could help me with the gaping pain I felt. I felt so lost. I just wanted to give up.

Jesus was always there for me. I was aware of His presence. It was during that time that I read the Bible eagerly day and night. The Lord spoke to me, giving me reason and courage to wake up the next morning and to live another day.

He promised me that *"He would do something new."* He promised me that He would make something out of what seemed impossible. That was my hope. During this time, I discovered two things which seemed impossible, but have since come true.

One main reason I chose to attend Biola was their offer for students to join Gospel Teams for preaching and outreach. I was nineteen, had told my story countless times, but had no consistent opportunities to preach. I knew the Lord would grant me the gifts and experiences to do what He had called me to do. I was compelled to preach the Gospel, although untrained.

I arrived in Westwood near UCLA with my friend Nicholas Woods. We were both burdened to see people know the love of Christ. I remember standing on a newspaper stand preaching Campus Crusade's *Four Spiritual Laws* Gospel tract which I had memorized. Seeds of the Word were planted, but we were scoffed at. I desired to learn how to preach more effectively and to engage people in what I believed to be the most important message of eternal significance.

I met a man named Jim Kirkpatrick, a Gospel preacher with the Open Air Campaigners (OAC) missionary organization. He invited me to join them for a Gospel meeting. The first night out, the Spirit opened the way for me to lead a man to Christ. It was the beginning of five years in ministry and training under the leadership of Area Director Russ Hodder.

I first preached the Gospel with OAC at Newport Beach. I knew it was the fulfillment of my call. The Spirit allowed me to preach with unusual freedom to over fifty adults who were awaiting entrance to a night club. The acoustics were good and the weather was cool. Numerous people responded to the invitation. I was asked to preach the same message again.

Weekly, for five years, I preached in public thoroughfares such as Westwood, Hollywood, Santa Monica, Hermosa Beach, Redondo Beach, Seal Beach as well as the ghettos in East Los Angeles and Santa Ana, California. People responded to the invitation almost every time one was given. It has been a testimony of the saving power of the Gospel. I also preached in Hawaii at Waikiki and at the Fort Street Mall when I returned during summer or winter breaks from school. I participated with Thomas Hoaeae, who though confined to a wheel chair refused to let his condition stop him from active street evangelism. The Lord used us to plant seeds of the Gospel as well as lead people to the Savior.

In the midst of this progress of purpose, I continued to have bouts with disillusionment and depression. Pastor Stanley Johnson and my father were able to listen to me when I poured out my frustrations of the spiritual walk and ambitions to preach Christ. I had often asked myself, "Why do I have to go to school? God has called me to preach the Gospel of Jesus Christ." I wanted to quit school with the immature and unrealistic notion that I would immediately preach to thousands. The Holy Spirit later showed me the importance of the training and character building.

On one visit to Saratoga, California, I spent a weekend with Pastor Johnson and his wife, June. He invited me to his office and opened his library which contained voluminous sets of Christian classics. He asked me to take whatever books I wanted. It was like being invited to take as much gold as I desired out of a priceless treasure chest. I took freely and left with deep feelings of gratitude, humility and responsibility. I asked him recently, why he invited me to take his books during such a low time in my life. He said, "I have to say it was the leading of the Spirit."

The second discovery that came during those lonely years was that the Lord opened my heart to a young woman whom I knew from my youth. We had grown up in the church and had sung in the Na Leo Nani O' Kalihi choir led by Dorothy Yuen.

Jamie Tokuda, the daughter of Ronald and June Tokuda, was a wholesome and pure person with a "gentle, quiet spirit." A beautiful Japanese woman with features which perfectly complemented her tender, sincere, and soft personality. We began dating. Because of my insecurity and lack of faith, I chose to be selfish, not considering the hurt I would cause, and broke off our growing relationship twice. She remained my friend and was always there for me when I was down, depressed and hurting and needed someone with whom to talk.

She understood me and she loved me. As a preacher, I was unlike most young men in that my thoughts, desires, and perspectives were characterized with a "Conquer the world for Christ" attitude which at times came across overwhelming, even cocky, blended with perplexing feelings of intense inadequacy to preach. Jamie seemed to have a God given ability to understand and bring out the best in me. These things took place in those first three years where I struggled to make friends, struggled to find my identity, and struggled to survive emotionally and socially.

We maintained our relationship as friends for four years until the Lord made it clear to me that she was the woman He created for me to marry. He reproved me for my selfishness and reminded me that I must also be the person she needed in order to meet her needs as well.

V

Called through Godly Influences
神の導きの中から

But you shall receive power when the Holy Spirit has come upon you; and you shall be witnesses to Me in Jerusalem, and in all Judea and Samaria, and to the end of the earth.
ACTS 1:8

Aka, e loaa no ia oukou ka mana, ke hiki mai ka Uhane Hemolele maluna iho o oukou; a e lilo auanei oukou i poe hoike no'u ma Ierusalema, a ma Iudea a pau, a ma Samaria, a hiki wale aku i ke kihi a ka honua.
OIHANA I:8

Preaching continued week after week in the open air and in addition to addressing crowds I gained special experience in dialogue, one-on-one with people from a wide range of backgrounds.

The following three years saw growth in my time spent to cultivating many deep friendships. I became more accepting of people who were different from me and found that they were willing to accept me, too. I began to make friends who would be my companions in ministry for a life-time.

In the last semester of studies at Biola University, I was granted early acceptance to the Talbot School of Theology for a Master's degree in Bible Exposition. One part of the requirements for the degree was fulfilled in a month's study tour to Egypt and Israel led by Dr. Ronald Pierce, Head of the Old Testament Department of Biola. I was exposed to archaeologists and authors such as David Dolan and Naim Ateek who kept abreast with the tumult in the Middle East from specialized perspectives. We traveled the Exodus route from Egypt to Sinai and from Sinai through the wilderness wanderings to Eilat (the southern most city in Israel) and to Galilee up to Rosh Hanikrah in the north.

The Bible came alive to me and the Gospel was further set in my heart as the need of the world. Visiting two sites where tradition claims Christ was raised from the dead left me speechless. I realized in a profound way that Jesus Christ is alive! It validated all His claims. He is the only person who died for the sins of mankind and was raised from the dead to live forever. There is no Gospel like the message of forgiveness and peace with God through Christ! My preaching would be changed forever.

My time at Biola and Talbot gave me exposure to Bible expositors and missionary statesmen from all over the world. I was able to speak to and receive personal encouragement from men such as Chuck Swindoll who told me to read widely, J.I. Packer from Britain who referred me to old books such as Matthew Henry's Commentary, Oswald Sanders of Overseas Missionary

Fellowship who gave me examples of the importance of prayer, George Verwer who gave me my first cassette of Dr. Martyn Lloyd Jone's preaching, Rev. Suksu Kim who took me weekly to the Prayer Mountain, and many other men and women of God who made an indelible influence on me for the ministry of Christ.

As I looked at the map of the world on my wall, I was reminded of the need of the world. Billions of people are dying without Christ and I have been entrusted with the message that can save them. In my own homeland Hawaii, many of our people are without Christ and without eternal hope. I pleaded with God for the opportunity to preach to them. He assured me that more than the desire I have to preach, He desired to let me to preach. My heart burned to preach Christ.

P

Picture day for Iolani School's football team. Brace on my left knee gives added support to my damaged cartilage and torn ligament.

M

My third year with Kalakaua Monarchs. I was already wearing #25 following in the footsteps of my father and brother.

I was teaching a small group about prayer at a winter camp for Japanese American Presbyterian churches in Southern California.

photo taken at SEARS in Buena Park, CA.

T

The last family portrait taken in 1991 the day before my graduation from Biola University.
Standing (L-R): me, David Jr.
Middle (L-R): Deva, my nephew, Kaloku and Iolani. Bottom (L-R): m
nephew, Keawe, my father, David Sr. and my mom, Eva.

The bottom of the Old Pali Road where I went for prayer. It was also the starting point of my infamous hike.

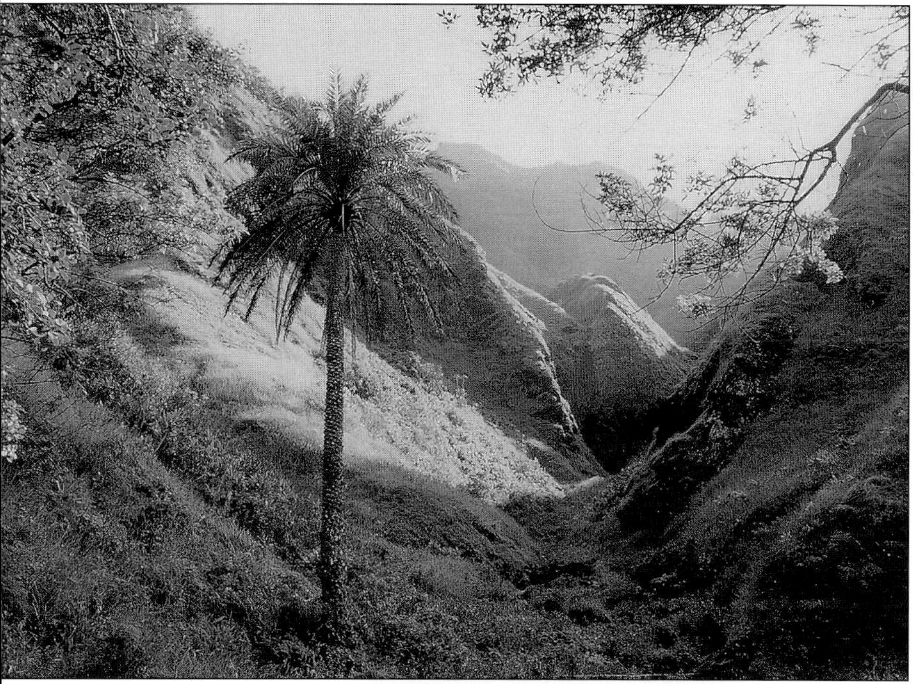

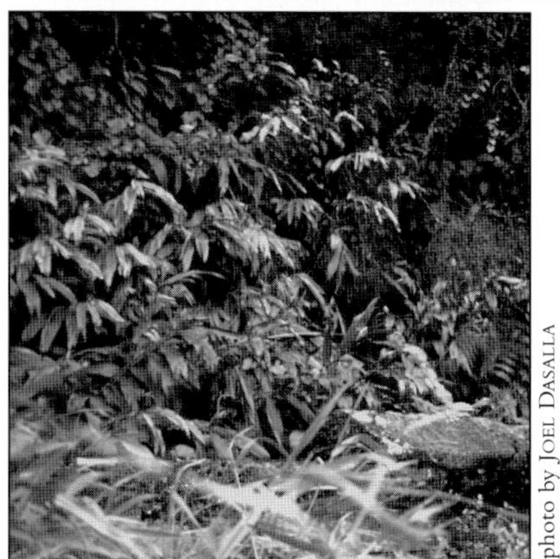

photo by Millie Yoshimoto

hoto by Joel Dasalla

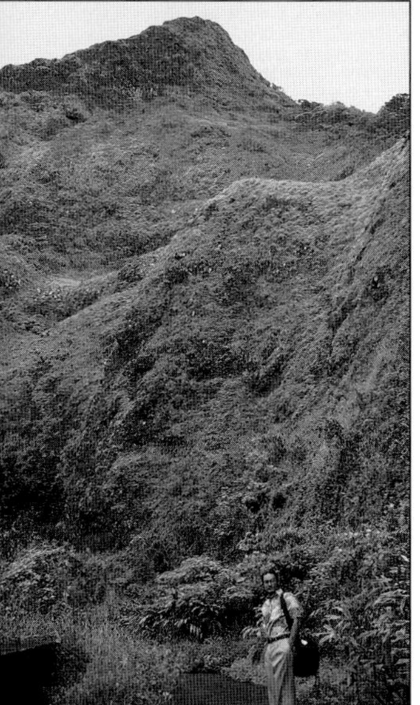

photo by Joel Dasalla

The ginger patch where I was found after the first 300-foot fall.

Pali fall put youth in Christ's hands

☐ Daniel Yamashiro was given a second chance to live his life with purpose

By Rod Ohira
Star-Bulletin

Eight years ago today, Daniel Yamashiro fell 400 feet from a ridge above the Pali Lookout and survived.

"It was a blessing," Yamashiro said, "because I was given a second chance to live a life with purpose."

That purpose, he says, is to deliver the word of Jesus Christ.

Yamashiro, 25, was ordained as a minister on Dec. 5 at Kalihi Union Church. His father David, 60, was ordained at the same time.

"The accident was the real turning point in my life," said Daniel, a football defensive back who had concluded a frustrating injury-plagued senior season for Iolani School about a month before the Pali fall.

"In high school, I was unable to live a devoted life because all I wanted to do was succeed in football," he said. "Playing football was the prime thought on my mind."

That changed after Yamashiro and a 16-year-old friend, Stacey Loui, went mountain climbing on a Sunday, three days before Christmas, in 1985. They were about 20 feet from the top when theLoui girl slipped.

Loui fell down a steep slope on the Kaneohe side of the "missing tooth" gap above the Pali Lookout.

"She landed on some trees and I was attempting to go down to help her when I slipped and fell over 300 feet," Yamashiro said. "I landed near the Lookout in a patch of ginger plants.

"It was a miracle I landed in the ginger patch because if it had been anywhere else, I would have fell to the road."

Loui managed to climb to the roadway and called police at about 7:20 p.m.

"I don't remember anything," Yamashiro said, "but I was told that when the rescue squad reached me, I moved and fell another 80 to 100 feet."

When rescue workers reached Yamashiro, he was alive but his head was split open.

"I had fractured my skull in two places and my scalp was ripped off," he said. "I had shattered my ankles, my organs were smashed and my body all cut up."

It took 70 stitches to close his head wound and plastic surgery erased most of the visible damage to his face. Incredibly, Yamashiro spent only three weeks in St. Francis Hospital.

"While I was in the hospital, I

See **FALL**, Page A-6

Newsclippings of my fall.

FALL: Youth was saved to serve

Continued from Page A-1

realized the Lord had saved me for a reason," he said. "But I didn't know what the reason was."

While his physical injuries mended quickly, the road to full recovery was tortuous.

"The emotional, social and psychological recovery took years," Yamashiro said. "My dream of playing football in college was shattered and my identity had changed.

"It was like looking at a different face in the mirror."

He was still struggling to piece his life back together when Yamashiro believes the Lord stepped in to lend a hand.

"I was driving over the Pali one night when I looked at the mountain where the accident had occurred," he said. "I knew then why I was saved.

"The spirit called on me to preach Jesus Christ. My purpose and direction changed at that moment."

David Yamashiro, who played football for the legendary Father Kenneth Bray at Iolani and later served as his son's position coach in the same sport, was inspired by Daniel's emotional turnaround.

"I've seen his life change from a broken person to what he is today," David Yamashiro said. "After the accident, he went from a person people used to look up to, to one that felt like he was a nobody.

"It was a miracle he survived the fall and I believe the hand of God was on Danny to give him a purpose for living."

Daniel Yamashiro spent a semester at Chaminade and transferred to Biola University, where he earned a degree in biblical studies and theology. He received his master's degree in bible exposition from Talbot Theological Seminary, a graduate school of Biola University.

Daniel Yamashiro preached five years on California streets as an evangelist for the Open Air Campaigners Missionary Organization.

He also served three years as a pastoral minister with Christ Presbyterian Church in Hollywood before returning to Hawaii.

"The first time I preached for the Open Air Campaigners, I knew that's the reason I'm alive," Daniel Yamashiro said. "Preaching is my calling."

He is president of the "Jesus Christ Is Calling You" Evangelistic Ministry, which has an outreach program including weekly street meetings at the Fort Street Mall, Waikiki and at the University of Hawaii.

A tent meeting is also being planned around Easter at Kapiolani Park.

David Yamashiro worked for the state Department of Housing and Urban Development and the Federal Housing Administration before retiring in 1985.

"I took an early retirement to attend seminary," he said. "When the accident happen, it just delayed my plans."

In 1990, he and his wife sold their condominium and moved to the mainland so David Yamashiro could complete his studies to become a minister.

David Yamashiro serves as an associate minister and handles adult education counseling at Kalihi Union Church.

He also visits with prison inmates weekly.

Faith has provided the Yamashiros with a strong life line.

In early January, they will pull together once again as David's wife, Eva, will undergo a kidney transplant operation in San Francisco.

Eva's donor will be her daughter, Iolani, a teacher at Kamehameha School.

David and Daniel Yamashiro, left to right kneeling, were both ordained at Kalihi Union Church earlier this month. Pastor Gerald Sanders spoke during the ordination service.

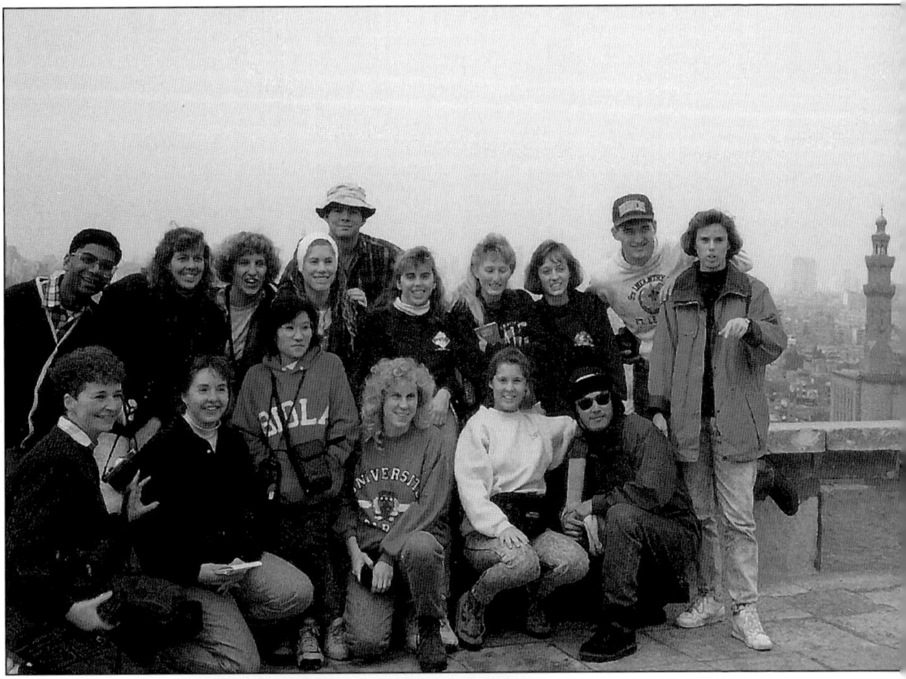

My 4th year
picture in the
Biola yearbook,
Biolan.

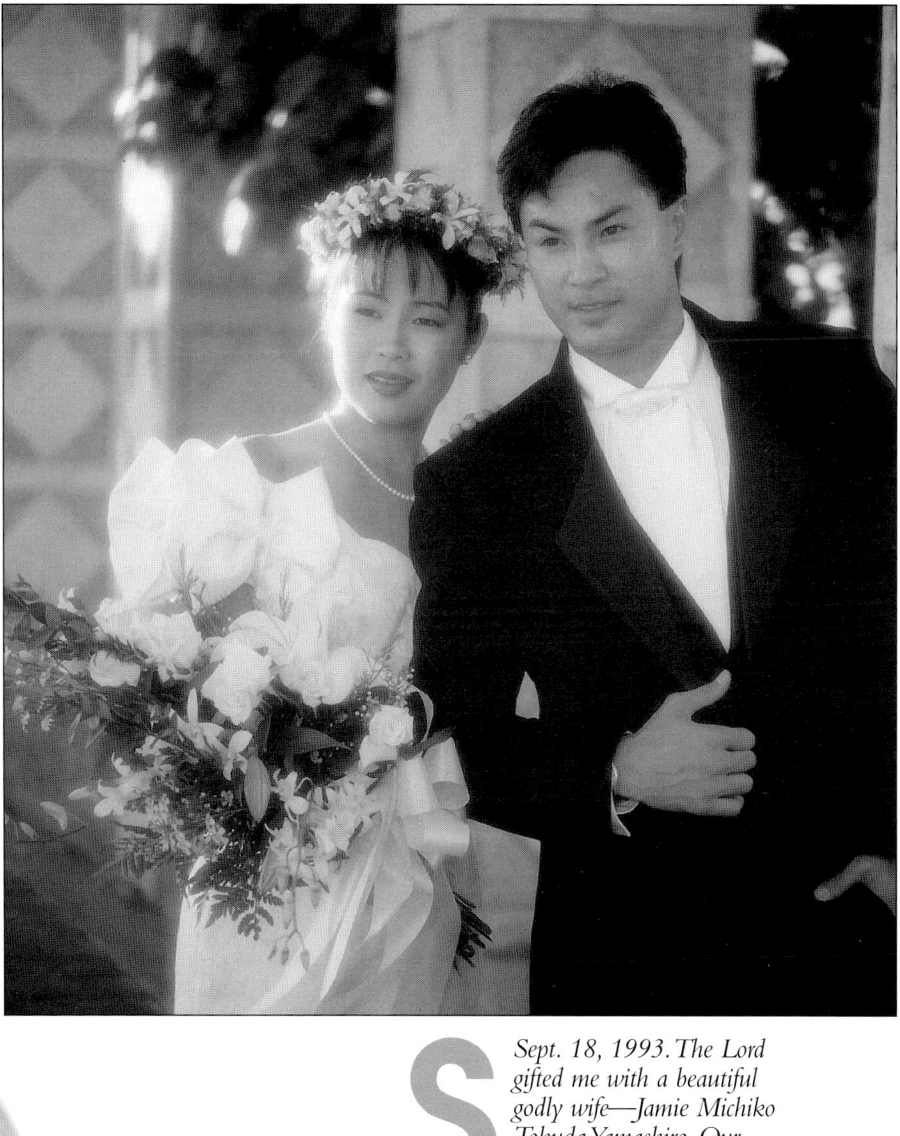

Sept. 18, 1993. The Lord gifted me with a beautiful godly wife—Jamie Michiko Tokuda Yamashiro. Our wedding portrait, taken in Honolulu, Hawaii.

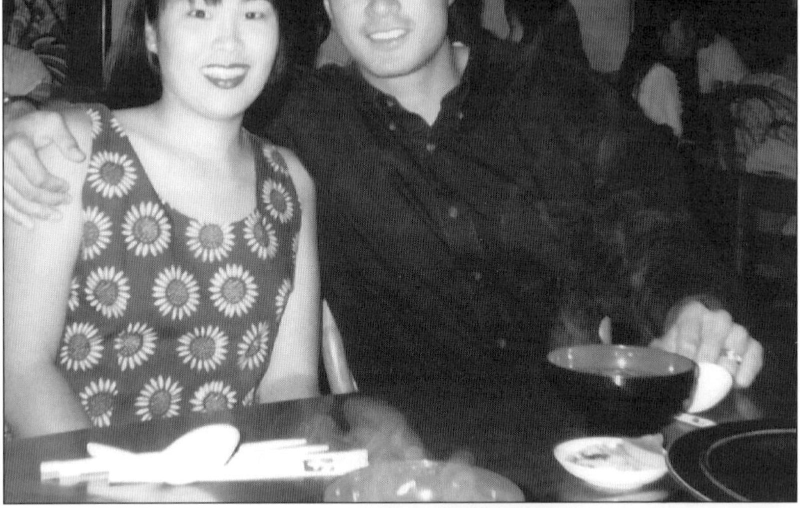

J

Jamie and I enjoy a relaxing dinner during our honeymoon in September of '93.

photo by OLAN MILLS

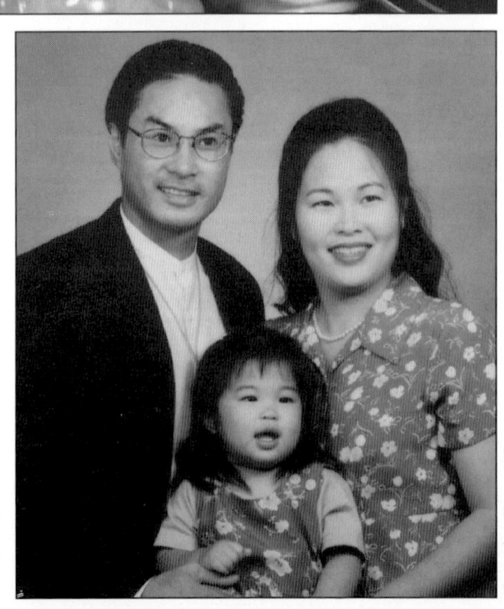

A

A family portrait: Allie is just a little over one year old.

I give a word of encouragement and thanksgiving
during my ordination at Kalihi Union Church,

photo by SUMIKO HENNA

A *At the conclusion of my ordination, this picture was taken. (L to R) Rev. Ted Esaki, Dr. Stanley Johnson, my mom—Eva Yamashiro, June Johnson, me, Jamie, and my father—Rev. David Yamashiro.*

Precious opportunity: I speak with international evangelist Dr. Luis Palau at NACIE '94.

Dr. John Corts, president of the Billy Graham Evangelistic Association (BGEA), instructed evangelists on administrative principles at NACIE '94.

A rare moment: I stand with Dr. Stephen Olford, his wife, Heather and son, Dr. David Olford in Memphis, TN at the Institute for Biblical Preaching.

H*Hugh Dunn and I preparing for the start of Tent Crusade No. 2 at Kapiolani Park in Hawaii's famous Waikiki.*

P *Preaching at the Kalihi Crusade in the Farrington Auditorium.*

GALLERY

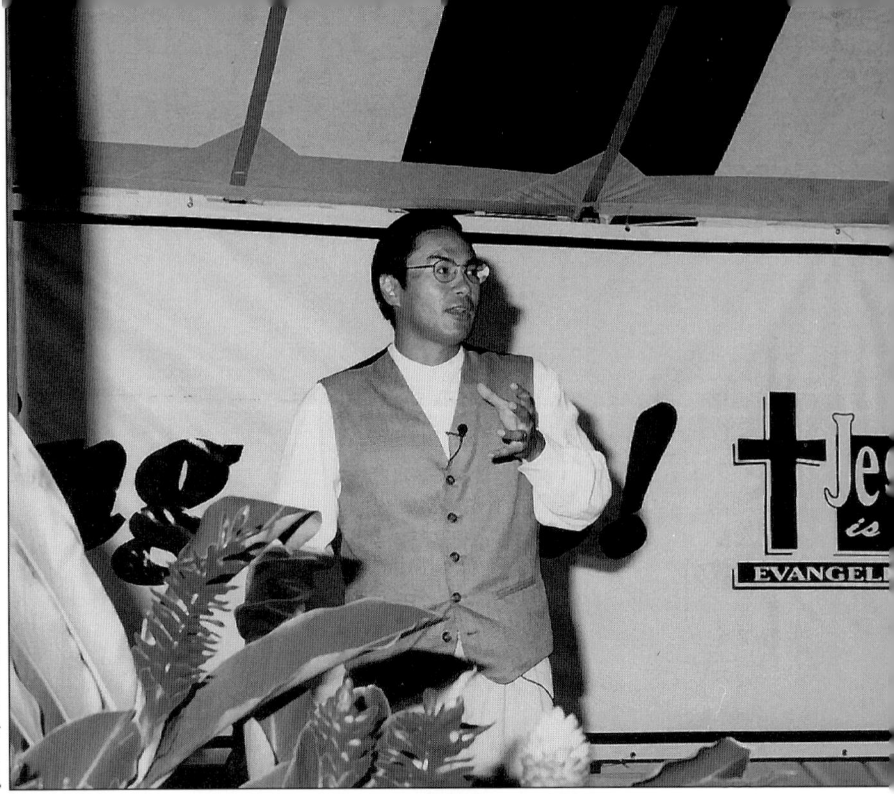

A *...at Central O'ahu Crusade in Mililani.*

J The JCCY Staff:
Danny, Dennis Frahm,
Waynette Shindo and
James Chappell

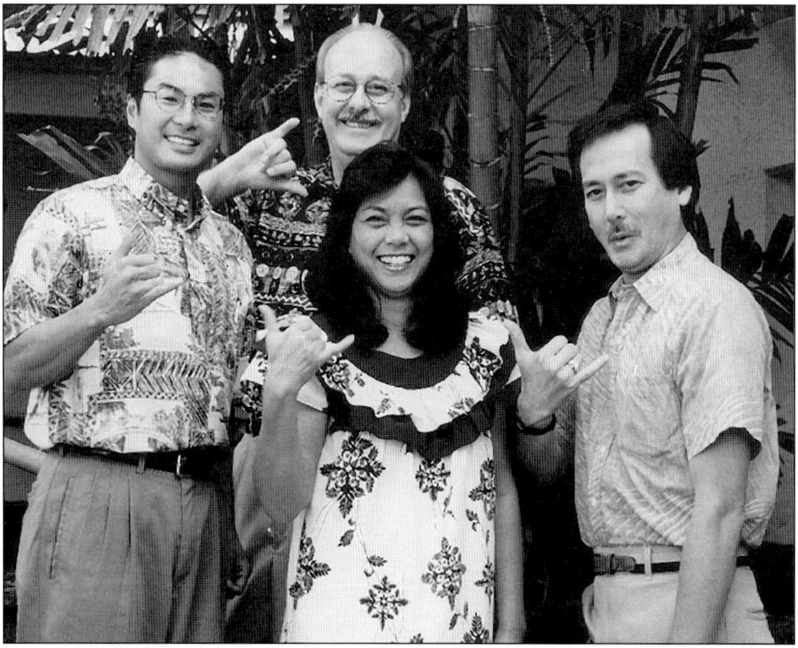

B *Billy Graham Twin Cities Crusade in Minneapolis, MN. Here are in the Press Box of the Metrodome: Hugh, James, Dennis and me.*

VI

Called to the Vision

ヴィ　ジョン

And He said to them, "Go into all the world and preach the gospel to every creature."
MARK 16:15

I mai la oia ia lakou, E hele aku oukou i na aina a pau, e hai aku i ka Euanelio i na kanaka a pau.
MAREKO XVI:15

I began to sense a greater burden to reach the lost with the message of Christ. The Lord confirmed the desire He laid on my heart at the age of eighteen to preach the Gospel to people around the world. First, I needed to start in Hawaii.

In 1993 I returned to Hawaii after five years in Los Angeles where I pastored for two years as an intern at Christ Presbyterian Church of Hollywood under the leadership of the Reverend Ted Esaki. I was called as a pastoral intern to Kalihi Union Church where I was under the tutelage of Dr. John Boaz. Much time was given to me for study and preaching preparation. This allowed me lengthy quiet moments of prayer and meditation.

One afternoon in March of 1993 my desire to preach was taken by the Holy Spirit and He led me to write five pages of details to a vision for evangelism that would start from Hawaii and eventually reach the world. As I wrote vigorously, there were details to the vision that only the Holy Spirit could enable. We were going to reach places of which I had never dreamed. I did not let any one see the vision except my sister, Iolani and Jamie, who was then my fiancee.

Seven months later, after I had been married in October of the same year, I was reading a textbook that was required for my studies in Expository Preaching at Trinity Theological Seminary in Newburgh, Indiana. The book was entitled *A Passion For Preaching* compiled by Dr. David Olford, the son of renowned evangelist and expositor Dr. Stephen Olford. In the chapter "Preaching" by Paul B. Smith, he said, "The church of Jesus Christ has a bigger job to do than any political party, and it is a mystery to me how any intelligent person can conclude that the mammoth task of reaching the entire world can be done on a one-to-one basis." I must say, that I am not of the persuasion that mass evangelism is the only way to reach people for Christ. In fact, it is on the one-to-one basis that makes mass evangelism effective. I am convinced that neither mass evangelism nor small group or one-to-one evangelism has the corner on methodology. All must be employed both strategically and complementarily. Smith went on to say, *"Theoretically, all Christians should be active witnesses, but that is simply not the case. Sometimes there is a lack of dedication, but often personal characteristics make it difficult for some Christians to share their faith with others. This leaves the church in the same position as most other organizations—limited to a minority of dedicated salesmen. If the multitudes are to be reached, we will always need specialists who can communicate with the masses, whether from the pulpit, through television, by radio, or the printed page. But only a person who refused to face the facts of the expanding population would attempt to dismiss the preacher as a relic of another generation."*

"To say that the Christian church should be different from every organization in this respect is sheer nonsense. It is quite obvious from the records that both Jesus and His disciples were not content to limit themselves to personal confrontations but continually took their stand in front of the largest crowds they could gather."[1]

While reading those words, there was a deep sense prompted by the Holy Spirit that the Lord would raise a mass evangelistic ministry out of Hawaii. The task would include first evangelizing Oahu and then reaching out across the neighbor islands and eventually to the world.

About one week had passed and I shared only with Jamie how the Spirit was moving in my heart. Then, I asked my friend Todd Dixon, a faithful Christian friend whom I grew up with, to have lunch with me at the Palace Saimin restaurant in Kalihi. I spoke to him about the burden and vision the Lord put on my heart. Todd was open to listen and even as I spoke, I could see his response was a confirmation of how the Lord was directing. He encouraged me to write some specifics which would be helpful in sharing the vision with key individuals.

As we parted, I knew I needed to be alone to hear from the Lord. I sat at my office desk for two hours as the Lord enabled me to draft a detailed presentation of the ministry answering anticipated questions that concerned people would ask. I drove home and worked for another two hours to format the presentation adequately. I shared it with my father, Todd, and our Senior Pastor Dr. John Boaz. They all confirmed that the vision was from the Lord and they encouraged me to pursue sharing it with key leaders.

The Lord taught me that He would reveal more of His vision at appropriate times so that I would have to depend on Him. We were directed to form a Prayer Team. I had been developing a Prayer Group over the course of that year and most of the members joined in the Prayer Team. We desired to include others from various churches as well. The responsibility of the Prayer Team was to pray daily for the ministry and meet on a regular basis to pray for the Evangelistic Tent Meetings we were to have. Over time, He opened doors to preach at other churches as well as meet with other pastors. Our first crusade was scheduled for April of 1994. We were not incorporated, we did not have a lawyer, and we had no money.

During this period of the ministry's inception, I was

ordained as a minister of the Gospel with my father
(who, though retired, at the age of 60 had recently
graduated with honors from Talbot School of Theology
in California the same time that I did). Among the pastors and leaders who made up the ordination commit-
tee were, the Rev. Dr. E. Richard Bartosik, then interim
at International Baptist Church, the Rev. Dr. John Boaz
and the Rev. David Oldfather of Kalihi Union Church,
the Rev. Calvin Chinen of Moanalua Gardens
Missionary Church, the Rev. Gerald Sanders of The
Church At Our House in Mililani, the Rev. Michael
Angevine of Makiki Christian Church, the Rev. Mark
Olmos of Faith Christian Fellowship, Mr. Rod Franklin,
Executive Director of the Bible Institute of Hawaii,
both Kenneth Takushi and Steven Kawamura, elders at
Kalihi Union Church. Two pastors flew to Hawaii from
California to speak at the ordination, the Rev. Dr.
Stanley Johnson, Pastor Emeritus of Saratoga Federated
Church and the Rev. Ted Esaki from Christ
Presbyterian Church of Hollywood.

An article of the unique event was published on the front page of the Honolulu Advertiser by Rod Ohira. Considerable coverage was given to the Lord's miraculous work in saving me from the 400-foot-fall and His call on my life to preach the Gospel.

The vision included a strategy for reaching the people of Oahu and the rest of Hawaii using the portable advantage of tents in which to gather crowds around the Hawaiian islands. We realized that it was not an original idea. It was an idea that had been almost forgotten. We agreed on this revisiting of the past and a rustic, austere motif for preaching the Gospel. It was a novelty for most who came into contact with our presentation.

We believed that the high-gloss effect of ministry, though effective in some instances needed to be played down in the early years of our establishment for the purpose of simplicity, focus and the character building process of tenacious perseverance. In our desire to reach people for Christ we desired to keep the ministry's colors black and white with a logo that boldly represented the cross on which Christ died. My philosophy was that black and white would stand out if used properly.

I started meeting with each of the elders of my church personally. We learned that the outreach ministry would be inter-denominational which would require me to network with churches and pastors from all over the state. The Lord directed me to attorney Damon Yonashiro who had invited me to speak to a group of business people in downtown Honolulu. I met with him beforehand and he asked me to share the vision with the Christian business group. One man there was Mr. Hal Jones, a former missionary and director of Campus Crusade for Christ Hawaii, a former legislator and then the President of Coldwell Banker and McCormick. He shared his testimony when we held our first tent meeting in Waikiki.

Damon responded to God's direction and recognized that it was the Lord's ministry. He graciously donated his services to file papers officially to incorporate the ministry as a non-profit organization and to prepare the forms for us to receive tax-exemption status.

The next task was to gather the Board of Directors. I did not look far as prominent leaders who would give the ministry instant credibility were already close to me. After much prayer and waiting the Lord led us to chose Ada Lum, a Bible teacher and author from the Bible Institute of Hawaii, Dr. John Boaz, the Senior Pastor of Kalihi Union Church; Mr. Elvin Lee, the Director of Finance at First Chinese Church; Randy Hongo, Na Hoku Hanohano award winner and President of Christian Vision; Thomas Masaki, a retired Insurance Executive; and the Rev. David Yamashiro Sr., Associate Pastor of Adult Education of Kalihi Union Church. They all sensed God's heart and responded to the invitation.

It was clear that even the title of the ministry needed to preach Christ. The name of the ministry would be, Jesus Christ is Calling You! Evangelistic Ministry, Inc. (JCCY). While still being incorporated in October of 1993, it was necessary for the ministry to produce material for presentation. So the Lord led me to write a simple Gospel tract and a five week discipleship book called *Welcome Christian: A Simple Study to Help You Walk with Jesus* which would be used at our Tent Meetings. Since then, the Rev. Rick Lazor of Nuuanu Baptist Church formatted the book along with the catchy drawings of illustrator Garrett Omoto. We also put together our ministry display and brochures which would let people know the foundations of our ministry and our statement of faith.

On April 14, 15, and 16 of 1994, we held our first crusade at Kapiolani Park at the edge of Waikiki. We started without money and were forced to trust God to provide for the needs of the ministry. At the time, I had determined not to ask for donations. This would be God's confirmation that it was His ministry and that He would sustain it. Todd Dixon and I were invited to speak for an hour about the ministry on Phillis Ramia's Heartlight television program.

I was also invited to an interview on KAIM radio station with its station manager Del Gibbs. We were able to produce posters and flyers and circulate them to numerous churches. We purchased air time on Hawaii's most listened to station KSSK, as well as advertisements of the Tent Meeting in *Midweek* newspaper, the *Honolulu Advertiser* and *Star Bulletin*.

Various churches joined us for that outreach. Randy and Gay Hongo were the worship leaders and each night we had special guests sharing their testimonies. Hal Jones, spoke on Thursday, State Senator Stan Koki testified on Friday, and 1988 Olympic Judo Champion Kevin Asano gave his story on Saturday. Each night the Prayer Team led by Faye Gibo and Aileen Asato were at the Park one hour early circling the tent and praying. Dennis and Jeanette Frahm and Alvin Kawazoe had trained over one hundred counselors and were ready for ministry to the needs of respondents to the invitation to receive Christ. Calvin Nakano had trained the Ushers who were greeting and seating the people. On Thursday night we saw a crowd of nearly 250 people. On Friday night there were over 350 people, and on Saturday there were over 500 individuals in attendance. Thirty persons were added to the kingdom. We received over $20,000 in donations. The ministry was confirmed as from the Lord.

VII

Called to Faithfulness

忠実であること

"... being confident of this very thing, that He who has begun a good work in you will complete it until the day of Jesus Christ.
PHILIPPIANS 1:6

Ua maopopo ko'u manao i keia mea, o ka mea nana i hoomaka i ka hana maikai iloko o oukou, nana no ia e hoomau a hiki i ka la o Iesu Kristo.
PILIPI I:6

The Lord has opened avenues for training and ministry expansion. Following the first Crusade, Jamie and I were invited to attend the North American Conference for Itinerant Evangelists (NACIE '94) where over 2,000 traveling evangelists and their spouses gathered in Louisville, Kentucky. It was sponsored by the Billy Graham Evangelistic Association (BGEA). We were exposed to the highest quality training for mass evangelistic preaching ministries today. We were privileged to hear the revered evangelist Dr. Billy Graham speak about the work of evangelistic preaching.

I attended seminars on administration, prayer, and discipleship. Jamie sat in on seminars for wives of evangelists. We both grew in our understanding of how the Lord God was investing in our lives for the sake of preaching the Gospel to Hawaii and eventually the world. We felt a sense of destiny as we asked ourselves, "Why did the Lord send us here to be with these people from across America and Canada, to hear preachers such as Dr. Graham, Dr. Luis Palau, Chuck Colson, Dr. Stephen Olford, Dr. Adrian Rodgers, and Dr. E.V. Hill.

I learned that there are two kinds of preaching evangelists. One is the denominational evangelist and the other is the inter-denominational evangelist. The denominational evangelist is supported largely by the denomination, and is primarily expected to preach in the denominational circles. The inter-denominational evangelist is a central catalyst for all denominations to do outreach and is unlimited in expansion and support.

I also learned the importance of building a financial base for the ministry JCCY. The Lord's resources are unlimited. I needed to be open to how He would provide the funds. We would need to extend our borders and build relations with denominations and their leaders as well as minister to lay people in the different areas, equipping the people for outreach. The financial support would come from individuals to whom we were ministering. Financial growth would help us build a paid staff who in turn would work in mobilizing countless people with the message of salvation through Christ.

A greater burden was felt as we grew more aware that the Lord was equipping us to work with others to do the ministry of evangelistic preaching in Hawaii and the world. I needed to be faithful and obedient to him, learning and applying what he had taught me.

Following NACIE 1994 Jamie who was pregnant with our daughter Allie returned to Hawaii as I remained in Memphis, Tennessee to study under the famed Bible Expositor Dr. Stephen Olford. He was trained under preaching professor W. Graham Scroggie, one of the early preachers at the Metropolitan Tabernacle, London after the "Prince of Preachers" Charles Haddon Spurgeon. Never as a youth had I dreamed of having the privilege to study with the man, 76 years old who spent over 50 years of his life preaching the Word of God throughout the world. He had become a bridge between the pulpiteers of Victorian England (1800's) from whom the Spirit of the Lord has taught and inspired me through their writing and preaching.

In Tennessee, I gathered with 20 other men from the world over. Experienced pastors of large churches and successful evangelists came recognizing the "once in a lifetime opportunity" to study with Dr. Olford. I roomed with the Reverend John James from Wales during three weeks of intensive homiletical (preaching) training with men from Africa, England, Canada, Russia, Australia, New Zealand, China, Taiwan, California, Pennsylvania, Maryland, Dallas, Minnesota, and Virginia.

We studied in depth, the art of expounding Scriptures with simplicity and by the Holy Spirit's unction. The Spirit of the Lord came down upon us after listening to the anointed instructions from the Word and we cried aloud together in desperation for the Spirit's power. Never before had I felt so inadequate to preach the most important message mankind can and will ever hear from God. It left me feeling utterly helpless and grateful as I became more deeply aware of my own sinfulness and need for God's grace.

As ministers and as men we bonded in the Spirit as the Lord made clear that He was preparing us for greater ministry and outreach in the future. Obviously, the worldwide contacts made there have been God given to expand the ministry beyond Hawaiian soil.

After our first crusade in Waikiki, it was obvious we needed additional administrative help for our upcoming Tent Meetings. James Chappell, who had both a willing spirit and practical experience in the church context joined the volunteer staff as Crusade Coordinator. We were on a learning curve. Neither James nor I had extensive experience in Crusade work. Following our second crusade in Waikiki, which resulted in a slight increase in attendance, we were aware that more strategic help was needed.

Shortly thereafter, I joined Hawaii local pastors for a Prayer Summit meeting at the St. Stephen's Diocesan Center. One of the facilitators was a man named Dave

Cetti who showed special interest in our ministry. He was for nearly twenty years the Crusade Coordinator for Evangelist Bob Cryder of Oregon. I expressed our need for training and he warmly invited James and me to spend several of the most profitable days. He met with James while I had practical lessons from Bob. After preaching that Sunday at Dr. Richard Lindemann's Sonrise Baptist Church, we returned home with ideas ready for implementation.

The JCCY Team developed specialists who gave valuable time laboring faithfully for the eternal well-being of people. Ed Shiroma and Faye Gibo were pillars in directing the Prayer Team. Todd Dixon handled all financial matters. James Chappell coordinated all events. Chris Tanaka, Lloyd Tokuda and Donald Hirai gave their expertise in leading crew members in logistics. Dennis Frahm with his wife Jeanette along with Alvin Kawazoe trained follow-up counselors for each crusade. Kim Yamauchi administered all marketing and advertising strategies. Cindy Aona and Cindy Okada worked with the graphic arts. Jenny Taoka edited newsletters. Jean Pacarro developed our neighborhood door to door canvassing capabilities. Calvin Nakano skillfully trained each greeter. Hugh Dunn became our very own Master of Ceremonies. Gloria Comorposa traveled countless miles distributing posters and flyers with her team. Arlene Iwano took care of data processing. Waynette Shindo help keep my schedule organized, and Yasuko Shiraishi, correspondence.

As of year end 1996 six crusade events have been conducted by JCCY having networked closely with over sixty churches from a spectrum of denominations. The Crusade ministry has enabled us the platform to communicate the Gospel on different locations on Oahu as well as directing us toward ministering with pastors to their congregations. We have seen churches become deeply burdened and committed to active relational, personal evangelism through the vehicle of practical pre-crusade training, culminating in the mass outreach event itself, and followed by discipleship emphases with new believers. Thousands have attended and hundreds have responded to Christ's call.

On April 30, 1996 my mother, who had suffered for five years of kidney failure and a weak heart went home to be with Jesus. Early that morning my father called and said, "Dan, Mom had a heart attack. We're at the Kaiser Hospital's emergency room." I fell to my knees. I knew my mother's health was deteriorating.

One of my greatest fears was to lose my parents. As a youth I had often said, "I wanted to die before them, not knowing how I would live without them." Now I was faced with a reality. I do not think anyone can be fully prepared for the loss of someone so dear. Jamie, and daughter Allie and I rushed to the hospital. Paramedic Wayne Yasutomi, a member of our church met me with tears in his eyes and said, "Danny, your Mom went home." I saw my father, we embraced and wept. I went to see my mother. I cried, holding her and looking up, prayed aloud, "Thank you, Lord, for loving and saving Mom's soul. I know she's with you now.

Thank you for sacrificing your life on the cross for her so that she could be forgiven of her sins and be your child for eternity." That experience instilled in me a greater sense of the pressing need to take Christ's message of hope to people. It made the urgency of the Gospel stronger than ever in my heart.

I was selected that summer to study with Dr. Leighton Ford in his Evangelism Leadership Seminar which was held on the campus of Fuller Theological Seminary. I was among thirty-two future leaders of world evangelization. Much inspiration was gained. Practical skills were acquired for leadership development, vision planning, implementation, administration, communication and methods of outreach.

One week later, I joined the members of the JCCY Team James Chappell, Dennis Frahm, Jeanette Frahm, and Hugh Dunn when invited to a special training with the Billy Graham Association in Minneapolis, Minnesota during their Twin Cities Crusade. We learned much about meticulous preparation as we witnessed, the supernatural phenomenon of seeing thousands respond to Christ's call.

We returned home and welcomed the Ambassador's Coalition, a budding missions training organization for high-school and college students under the direction of founder Mark Kim. Together, we have developed the JCCY School of Evangelism Summer Training Program. Each year students would arrive from California to receive instruction on the basic biblical principles for effective personal witnessing and given practical experience through daily outreaches in various contexts. Daily worship characterizes the agenda. Specialized training is given for street preaching. Drama is employed as a crowd gathering vehicle for Gospel communication. It has proven to be a God-given agent for missions and evangelism commitment during such volatile years of youth.

In January of 1996 we began our first daily radio broadcast *Jesus Is Calling You!* on KAIM. The purpose of the program was two fold: First, encourage and equip the Christian listeners in evangelism and second, engage the minds and hearts of pre-Christians with simple, practical, relational messages that direct them to consider Christ and His good news of hope.

A young lady was a college student in Hilo. After I preached in her church she said with a smile, "It's so good finally to put the face and the voice together." "Danny," she said, "Every night I listened to your program and it was enough to get me through the next day." Praise God for his Word!

In early 1994, with the help of Brian and Jan Lee of Dioko Productions, the *Jesus Is Calling You!* Tent Meetings were aired twice weekly on television and continue to the time of this writing. Tens of thousands are exposed to the Gospel every week in Hawaii. We have sent numerous follow-up packets over the last two years to people who have called us after receiving Jesus.

I was asked to host the *Prayerline Hawaii* weekly live broadcast on KWHE LeSEA Broadcasting. It is a program which allows us to feature special guests, deliver brief devotional, and minister to people who call in with prayer requests. Television and radio have given us the much needed exposure and credibility for church unity to labor side by side in the harvest field of Hawaii.

JCCY has focused on mobilizing large numbers of volunteers from participating churches to fulfill the many responsibilities necessary to minister with excellence. We have needed help to mobilize a growing number of volunteers. In 1996, two paid staff persons were added: Dennis Frahm, Church Relations and Follow-Up and Waynette Shindo, Secretary.

VIII

What Does This Mean to You?
あなたにとって重要なことは？

I hope that you were blessed, encouraged and inspired in reading this story. Maybe you have shared some of the pains and some of the joys with me. Perhaps you now desire to reach loved ones in your family and friends with the message of salvation through Christ. Let this book help you to put into practice what the Lord has taught you.

If you are a pastor or lay person who would like to be involved in the upcoming Paradise Crusades with the JCCY Ministry, you are welcomed. We have informational brochures to aide in your church planning as well as being available through telephone or letter correspondence.

It could be that you know of someone who would be interested in this special ministry of outreach and you would like that person to contact us. We shall look forward to hearing from them.

You may have read this story and it has moved you. You do not know Jesus Christ as your Savior and Lord. Your sins are not forgiven, and you know that if you were to die tonight, you would not be guaranteed entrance to heaven. My desire is that everyone who reads this story will hear Jesus Christ calling them and that they will respond to the invitation for salvation through Him. God is holy and we are sinful.[2] Without Christ, no person can know the God who created them because sin separates us from God.[3] But God shows His own love toward us in that while we were yet sinners, Christ died for us.[4] He was raised from the dead and the Bible says that each one of us must receive Him personally as Savior and Lord in order to make peace with God, become his children, and be granted entrance to heaven.[5] This requires confession of sin, repentance from sin and submission to God.[6] Jesus has made it possible for you and me to experience this ulti-mate blessing simply by putting your faith in him, receiving him into your heart. You are not reading these words by chance. You have been destined to read this book so that you may find peace with God through Jesus Christ right now. I encourage you to receive Him into your heart this moment.

I am going to lead you in a simple prayer. Pray this with me.

> *"Jesus, thank You for loving me. I know that You died on the cross for me. I am a sinner. Please forgive me of all my sins. I know that You are alive! Please come into my heart. I receive You as my Savior and Lord. I give my life to You. I desire to submit to You that Your life may be lived through me. Amen."*

If you said that prayer, you have become a born again believer.[7] Christ has come into your heart. If you do not have a Bible, get one and write on the first page the date and occasion of your new life in Christ. Write, "On ________ I received Jesus Christ into my heart as my Savior and Lord. I did this after the Spirit of God spoke to me when I read the book Paradise Calls. Now I know I am a Christian and am destined for heaven." Then sign your name.

The Bible says in 2 Corinthians 5:17, "Therefore, if anyone is in Christ, he is a new creation; old things have passed away; behold, all things have become new." Read 1 John 5:1-13. It is God's reminder that you are sure to go to heaven because you have Christ. Read the Bible daily.[8] Start from the book of Mark. Speak to the Lord every time the Spirit reminds you to pray.[9] Go find a church which is Christ-centered and preaches the Bible.[10] Do not stop until you find one.

Notes

1. Smith, Paul B., *"Preaching"* a chapter in the book compiled by David Olford, *A Passion for Preaching*, (Nashville: Thomas Nelson Publishers, 1989).
2. Romans 3:23
3. Romans 6:23
4. Romans 5:8
5. I Corinthians 15:3-4 and John 1:12
6. Romans 10:9-10 and Acts 2:38
7. John 3:5-8
8. Psalm 1
9. I Thessalonians 5:17
10. Hebrews 10:25

Books by Danny Yamashiro

Welcome Christian
A simple five part Bible study for the new believer

Jesus Christ in Every Biblical Book
A study of types, symbols, prophecies, figures and signs of Christ in Scripture

The Open Air Evangelist
Eye opening presentation of the preaching evangelist: man, message, method

Answer Their Questions
User friendly answers to questions frequently asked about Christianity